WHAT'S INSIDE A Radio?

Digital Clock Radio

AM
PM

BATTERY BACKUP

WAKE

FM 88   92   96   100 104 108   MHz

AM x10 55   65   80   100 130 160   KHz

ARNOLD RINGSTAD

childsworld.com

Published by The Child's World®
1980 Lookout Drive • Mankato, MN 56003-1705
800-599-READ • www.childsworld.com

Photographs ©: Rick Orndorf, cover (clock), 1 (clock), 4, 7, 9, 11 (top), 11 (bottom), 13, 14 (wheel), 15, 16 (speaker), 17 (top), 17 (bottom), 19, 24; Syafiq Adnan/Shutterstock Images, cover (screen), 1 (screen), 6 (screen), 18 (screen), 22 (screen); Shutterstock Images, cover (plug), 1 (plug), 2, 3 (plug), 3 (circuit board), 5 (glasses), 5 (scissors), 6 (wires), 8 (screw), 10, 12 (plug), 12 (circuit board), 16 (screw), 18 (circuit board), 20 (screw), 22 (circuit board), 23; Praiwun Thungsarn/Shutterstock Images, 3 (screwdriver), 5 (screwdriver), 8 (screwdriver), 14 (screwdriver), 20 (screwdriver); Shyripa Alexandr/Shutterstock Images, 5 (gloves)

ISBN 9781503832039
LCCN 2018962806

Printed in the United States of America
PA02419

About the Author

Arnold Ringstad lives in Minnesota. He likes
to listen to the radio while writing books.

Contents

Materials and Safety

Materials
- ☐ Phillips screwdriver
- ☐ Radio
- ☐ Safety glasses
- ☐ Scissors
- ☐ Work gloves

Safety

- Always be careful with sharp objects, such as screwdrivers.

- Unplug the radio and then cut its power cord before you start. Throw away the end of the power cord.

- Wear work gloves to protect your hands from sharp edges.

- Wear safety glasses in case pieces snap off.

Radio

Phillips screwdriver

Work gloves

Scissors

Safety glasses

Inside a Radio

Radios pick up **signals** from the air. Then they turn those signals into sound. Some people listen to music on the radio. Others listen to news or sports. How does a radio work? What's inside?

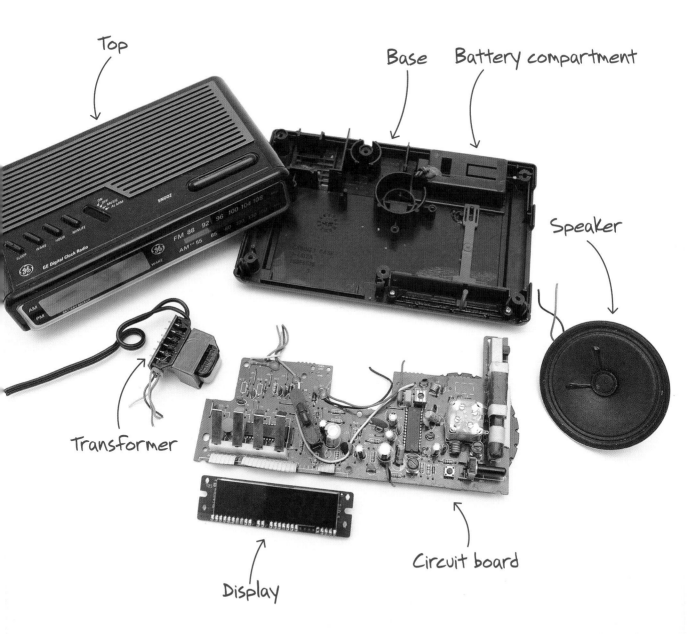

Top

Base

Battery compartment

Speaker

Transformer

Display

Circuit board

Opening the Radio

Several screws hold the outer case of the radio together. They are in the base. Remove them. Now you can pull the top off the base. Inside, you can see many parts. They include a **circuit board**, a speaker, a battery compartment, and a display.

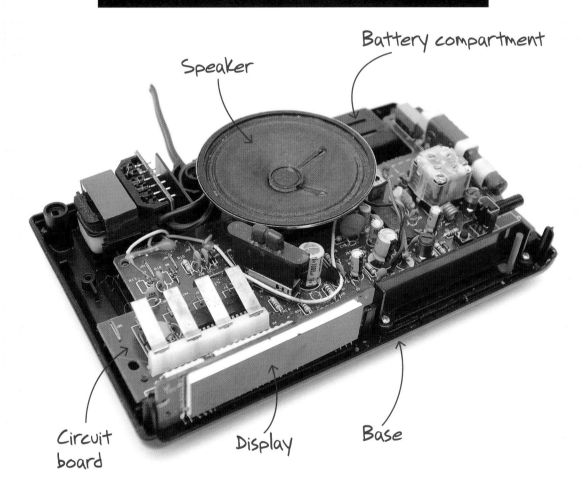

Battery compartment

Speaker

Circuit board

Display

Base

Getting Power

The radio needs electricity to work. Electricity enters through a cord in the back. It goes into a part called a transformer. The transformer turns the electricity into a form the radio can use. From here, the electricity goes into the circuit board.

A thick black power cord carries electricity into the transformer.

Thin, colorful cables carry electricity from the transformer into the radio.

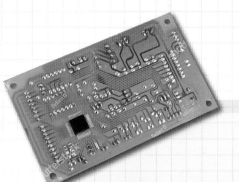

Receiving Signals

The radio's antenna is on the circuit board. The antenna is a rod with copper wire wrapped around it. It receives radio signals from the air. Then these signals go to the **capacitors**. The capacitors filter out the signals the user does not want.

Capacitors

Antenna

Circuit board

13

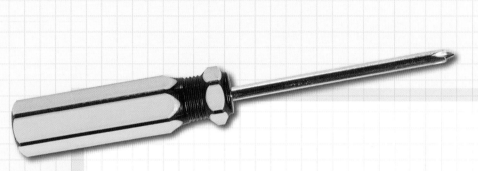

Picking a Station

There is a wheel on the radio's side. The user spins it to pick which signals he or she wants to hear.

Spinning the wheel moves an orange rod right or left.

This tells the capacitors to filter out all other signals. The wheel also moves a plastic rod in the front of the radio. The rod shows which **frequency** the user has picked. Every radio station has its own frequency. The frequency carries the radio station's signal.

Making Music

Next, the signals travel to a **microchip**. The microchip sends them to the speaker. Inside the speaker is a copper coil and a magnet. On the outside is a paper cone. When a signal goes to the speaker, the coil and magnet make the cone **vibrate** in a certain way. This creates sound.

Back of speaker

Front of speaker

Microchip

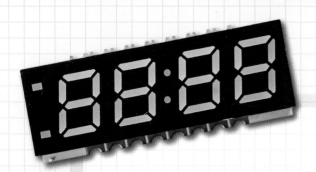

More Features

This radio does more than play music. The circuit board has a microchip that helps it tell time. There is a display to show what time it is. The radio also has switches to set an alarm or turn the alarm off. The radio packs many features into a small case.

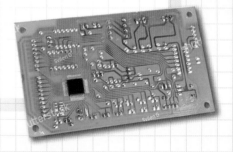

Microchip

Switches

Display

Reusing a Radio

We've taken apart a radio and learned what's inside. Now what? Here are some ideas for how to reuse the parts of a radio. Can you think of any more?

- **Circuit Board Display:** Mount the circuit board on a poster board. Try labeling the parts you can identify.

- **Storage Unit:** If you take the circuit board out and put the radio's top back on, the radio has lots of room inside. What can you store in there? Be creative!

Glossary

capacitors (kuh-PASS-uh-terz): Capacitors are parts that control the flow of electricity. Capacitors help filter out unwanted signals.

circuit board (SUR-kit BORD): A circuit board is a piece of material that holds computer chips, switches, and other parts. Inside the radio, many important parts are on the circuit board.

frequency (FREE-kwuhn-see): The frequency of something is how many times it cycles each second. Radio signals have a frequency of thousands or millions of times each second.

microchip (MY-kroh-chip): A microchip is a part that contains electrical circuits designed to do a certain job. In a radio, a microchip helps process signals.

signals (SIG-nuhlz) Signals are electrical pulses sent to radios. Radios turn signals into sound.

vibrate (VY-brayt): To vibrate is to shake back and forth quickly. The speaker vibrates to create sound.

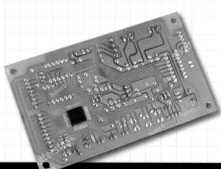

To Learn More

IN THE LIBRARY

Boothroyd, Jennifer. *From Typewriters to Text Messages: How Communication Has Changed*. Minneapolis, MN: Lerner Publishing Group, 2012.

Hall, Pamela. *Discover Sound*. Mankato, MN: The Child's World, 2015.

Holzweiss, Kristina. *Amazing Makerspace DIY with Electricity*. New York, NY: Scholastic, 2018.

ON THE WEB

Visit our website for links about taking apart a radio: **childsworld.com/links**

Note to Parents, Teachers, and Librarians: We routinely verify our Web links to make sure they are safe and active sites. So encourage your readers to check them out!

Index